# Table of Contents
## Grammar Grade 2

# Common Nouns (I)

A common noun names a person, place, or thing.

Fill in the circle below each common noun.

1. The boy took a bucket to the beach.
   ◯ ◯ ◯

2. His sister took a pail and a big umbrella.
   ◯ ◯ ◯ ◯

3. The children set their things on the sand.
   ◯ ◯ ◯

4. Then they began to build a sand castle.
   ◯ ◯ ◯

5. Other people waded in the surf.
   ◯ ◯ ◯ ◯

6. Two men flew big box kites.
   ◯ ◯ ◯ ◯

7. The lifeguard sat on a tall stand.
   ◯ ◯ ◯ ◯

8. It was a perfect day at the shore.
   ◯ ◯ ◯ ◯

# Common Nouns (II)

## A common noun names a person, place, or thing.

Circle the common nouns in each sentence.

1. My class gave a play for the whole school.

2. We had the performance in the gym.

3. One person was the storyteller.

4. A boy played the shepherd.

5. His job was to care for the sheep.

6. Four children were the sheep.

7. A wolf was after the animals.

8. The townspeople ran to help save the sheep.

9. The wolf was caught.

10. The audience cheered and clapped.

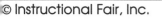

# Proper Nouns (I)

A proper noun names a special person, place, or thing. It begins with a capital letter.

Circle each proper noun.

1. Bambi

2. paper

3. John Kennedy

4. Monroe School

5. Ireland

6. library

7. North Carolina

8. Mr. Bishop

9. Sarah

10. Texas

11. South Pole

12. Aunt Sadie

13. Atlantic Ocean

14. Uncle Joe

15. Pecos River

16. principal

# Proper Nouns (II)

A proper noun names a special person, place, or thing. It begins with a capital letter.

Underline each proper noun.

1. George Washington never lived in Washington, D.C.

2. Philadelphia was the capital city back then.

3. Washington, D.C., became the capital of the United States later.

4. The city was built on the shores of the Potomac River.

5. The White House was finished in 1800.

6. John Adams was the first president to live there.

7. Famous pets like Socks and Millie have lived in the White House.

8. Thomas Jefferson had terraces added to the White House.

# Singular and Plural Nouns

A singular noun names one person, place, or thing. A plural noun names more than one person, place, or thing.

Write the nouns from the Word Box under the correct heading.

**Word Box**

| | | | |
|---|---|---|---|
| birds | brushes | collar | party |
| dress | friends | glass | stores |
| head | shoes | | |

| **Singular Nouns** | **Plural Nouns** |
|---|---|
| | |

# Plural Nouns (I)

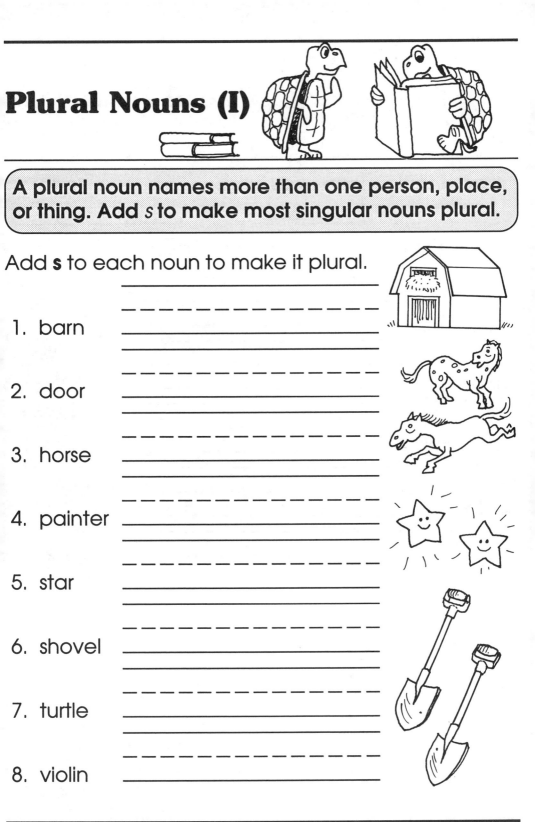

**A plural noun names more than one person, place, or thing. Add *s* to make most singular nouns plural.**

Add **s** to each noun to make it plural.

1. barn

2. door

3. horse

4. painter

5. star

6. shovel

7. turtle

8. violin

# Plural Nouns (II)

Add **-es** to each noun to make it plural.

1. buzz

2. ax

3. church

4. fox

5. lunch

6. bush

7. match

8. kiss

es

es

# Plural Nouns (III)

> **Add _s_ to make most singular nouns plural. If the noun ends in** _sh, ch, x, s, or z,_ **add** _-es._

Read the first sentence. Write the **plural** of the underlined noun in the blank in the second sentence.

1. My <u>class</u> went on a field trip yesterday.

   Several other _____ went also.

2. Our class got on one <u>bus</u>.

   There were four _____ in all.

3. We drove to the <u>zoo</u>.

   How many _____ have you visited?

4. First, we saw the new baby <u>elephant</u>.

   The other _____ watched the baby.

# Subject Pronouns (I)

**Subject pronouns replace nouns or noun phrases in the subject part of sentences.** *I, you, he, she, it, we,* **and** *they* **are subject pronouns.**

Write the pronoun that takes the place of the underlined words.

1. <u>My mother</u> is a clown!

   _____

   _ _ _ _ _ _ _ _ _ _ _ _ _

   _____ is a clown!

2. <u>Clowns</u> go to special schools.

   _____

   _ _ _ _ _ _ _ _ _ _ _ _

   _____ go to special schools.

3. <u>One school for clowns</u> is in Florida.

   _____

   _ _ _ _ _ _ _ _ _ _ _ _

   _____ is in Florida.

4. <u>One man</u> teaches a class there.

   _____

   _ _ _ _ _ _ _ _ _ _ _ _

   _____ teaches a class there.

5. <u>Dad and I</u> are proud of Mom.

   _____

   _ _ _ _ _ _ _ _ _ _ _ _

   _____ are proud of Mom.

# Subject Pronouns (II)

Subject pronouns replace nouns or noun phrases in the subject part of sentences. *I, you, he, she, it, we,* and *they* are subject pronouns.

Rewrite each sentence, replacing the underlined noun or phrase with the correct pronoun.

1. <u>Bats</u> are amazing animals.

_____

_____

2 <u>My sister</u> is afraid of bats.

_____

_____

3. <u>You and I</u> might see them.

_____

_____

4. <u>A bat</u> is very smart.

_____

_____

5. <u>My dad</u> says bats eat insects.

_____

_____

# Object Pronouns (I)

**An object pronoun replaces a noun or noun phrase in the predicate part of a sentence.** *Me, you, him, her, it, us,* **and** *them* **are object pronouns.**

Write the pronoun that takes the place of the underlined word.

1. Some animals need <u>tongues</u> in order to survive.

   _____

   — — — — — — — — — — —

   _____

2. A chameleon uses <u>the tongue</u> to catch food.

   _____

   — — — — — — — — — — —

   _____

3. Chameleons amaze <u>my brother</u>.

   _____

   — — — — — — — — — — —

   _____

4. The anteater amused <u>our class</u>.

   _____

   — — — — — — — — — — —

   _____

5. Anteaters eat <u>termites</u>.

   _____

   — — — — — — — — — — —

   _____

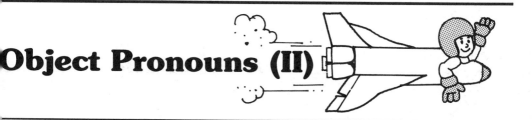

An object pronoun replaces a noun or noun phrase in the predicate part of a sentence. *Me, you, him, her, it, us,* and *them* are object pronouns.

Rewrite each sentence. Replace the underlined words with the correct object pronoun.

1. Please join <u>Jill and me</u> on a trip.

   _____

   _____

2. John told <u>Stan</u> to come also.

   _____

   _____

3. The shuttle carries <u>Jill and Stan</u>.

   _____

   _____

4. We see <u>thick clouds</u>.

   _____

   _____

5. The clouds trap <u>the solar energy</u>.

   _____

   _____

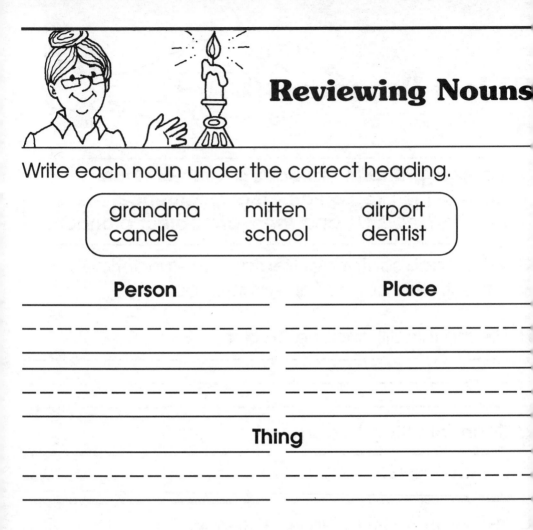

# Reviewing Nouns

Write each noun under the correct heading.

> grandma     mitten     airport
> candle     school     dentist

**Person**

**Place**

**Thing**

Write the plural of each noun.

1. tax

3. comb

2. chance

4. batch

# Reviewing Nouns and Pronouns

Circle the proper nouns in each sentence.

1. Neil Armstrong was the first man on the moon.

2. Edwin Aldrin was the second.

3. Michael Collins piloted the command module.

4. They went on their trip in July of 1969.

Write the correct pronoun to replace each underlined word or phrase.

1. <u>The mission</u> was called Apollo 11. _____

2. <u>Collins</u> stayed in the command module. _____

3. <u>Armstrong and Aldrin</u> were in the lunar module. _____

4. <u>My mother</u> watched them on T.V. _____

5. <u>My friend and I</u> study space. _____

# Action Verbs (I)

**An action verb shows action.**

Circle the action verb in each sentence.

1. Sara builds a sandcastle.

2. Steven plays in the water.

3. He splashes in the waves.

4. Nick runs on the beach.

5. Kyle swims in the lake.

6. He plays happily.

7. The family eats lunch.

8. They laugh together.

9. Eric finds a pretty rock.

10. He searches for more.

11. They walk along the beach together.

# Action Verbs (II)

An action verb shows action.

Underline the action verb in each sentence. Write it on the line.

1. Miguel and Rosita gathered some wood. _____

2. They took it to Papa. _____

3. Papa built a fire with the sticks. _____

4. Then he lighted the twigs. _____

5. Soon the fire blazed. _____

6. Papa peeled the bark of two green branches. _____

7. He gave each child one. _____

# Action Verbs (III)

**An action verb shows action.**

Circle the verb in the sentence. Write it on the line.

1. Carl ran to first base.  _____

2. Susie threw the ball to Paco.  _____

3. He jumped high into the air.  _____

4. Kara walked back and forth nervously.  _____

5. Sergi yelled for his team.  _____

6. Kara hit the ball hard.  _____

7. She ran quickly.  _____

# Linking Verbs (I)

A linking verb does not show action. It links the subject with a word in the predicate part of a sentence. *Am, is, are, was,* and *were* are linking verbs.

Write **am, is,** or **are** in each blank.

1. Reading _____ my favorite hobby.

2. I _____ a good reader.

3. Dad and I _____ glad we have a library nearby.

Write **was** or **were** in each blank.

1. I _____ happy to get two books for my birthday.

2. They _____ a gift from my dad.

3. The books _____ interesting.

# Linking Verbs (II)

A linking verb does not show action. It links the subject with a word in the predicate part of a sentence. *Am, is, are, was,* and *were* are linking verbs.

Write **am, is,** or **are** in each blank.

1. The monarch butterfly _____ amazing.

2. Its eggs _____ tiny.

3. I _____ a bug collector.

Write **was** or **were** in each blank.

1. I _____ interested in the chrysalis.

2. The butterfly's wings _____ wet.

3. The butterfly _____ wrinkled.

# Present Tense Verbs (I)

**Present tense verbs show action that is happening** *now.*

Write the verb that tells what is happening **now** in the blank.

1. The children _____ Alex.
   (watch, watched)

2. Alex _____ his presents.
   (opened, opens)

3. The dog _____ .
   (barks, barked)

4. Alex _____ for a new bike.
   (wished, wishes)

5. Mother _____ a cake.
   (bakes, baked)

6. Everyone _____ a game.
   (played, plays)

# Present Tense Verbs (II)

**Present tense verbs show action that is happening** *now.*

Circle each verb in the Word Box that tells what is happening **now**. Put an **X** on each word that does not.

| | | **Word Box** | | |
|---|---|---|---|---|
| bakes | yelled | come | cry | jumped |
| give | reached | hurts | needs | rides |
| sleeps | stretch | write | shares | smiled |
| goes | marches | skipped | looked | kicked |

Write the present tense verb in each sentence below.

1. The Alaskan Husky _____ happily.
   (barks, barked)

2. The four other dogs_____ closely.
   (follow, followed)

3. The dogs _____ a sled.
   (pull, pulled)

# Past Tense Verbs (I)

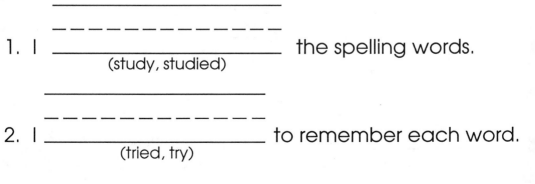

> Past tense verbs show action that has already happened.

Write the verbs that show **past** action.

1. tag
   tagged
   _____
   _____

2. carry
   carried
   _____
   _____

3. fry
   fried
   _____
   _____

4. trimmed
   trim
   _____
   _____

Write the verb that shows **past** action in each sentence.

1. I _____ the spelling words.
   (study, studied)

2. I _____ to remember each word.
   (tried, try)

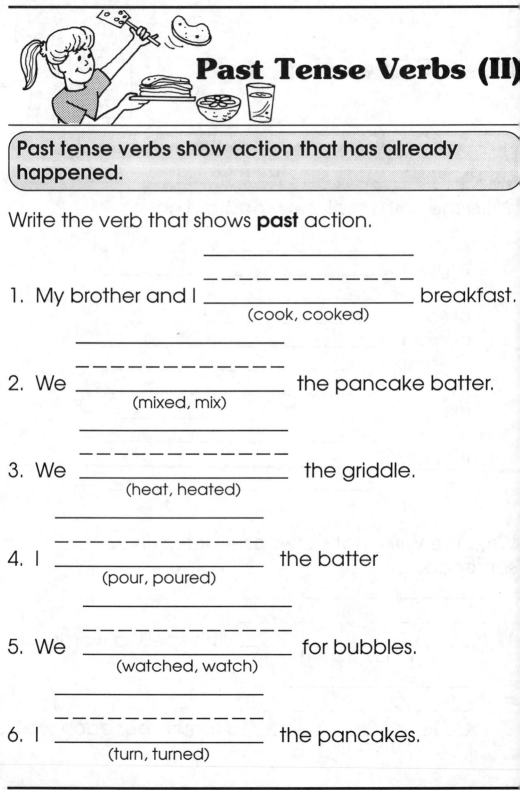

# Past Tense Verbs (II)

Past tense verbs show action that has already happened.

Write the verb that shows **past** action.

1. My brother and I _____ breakfast.
   (cook, cooked)

2. We _____ the pancake batter.
   (mixed, mix)

3. We _____ the griddle.
   (heat, heated)

4. I _____ the batter
   (pour, poured)

5. We _____ for bubbles.
   (watched, watch)

6. I _____ the pancakes.
   (turn, turned)

# Irregular Verbs (I)

Irregular verbs do not show past tense by adding -ed.

Circle the word that shows **past** action.

1. run,  runs,  ran

2. sees,  saw,  see

3. brought,  bring,  brings

4. drive,  drives,  drove

Write the **past** tense of the verb.

1. I _____ my mother's car.
   (see)

2. She _____ in the driveway.
   (drive)

3. We _____ to see her.
   (run)

# Irregular Verbs (II)

Irregular verbs do not show past tense by adding -ed.

Fill in the blank with the past tense of the verb.

1. Fido _____ a huge hole.
   (digs, dug)

2. Then he _____ because he was tired.
   (sleeps, slept)

3. Muffy then _____ along to cause trouble.
   (comes, came)

4. She _____ behind the dog house.
   (hides, hid)

5. Fido _____ aware of Muffy.
   (became, becomes)

6. Muffy's owner _____ her to behave.
   (told, tells)

# Irregular Verbs (III)

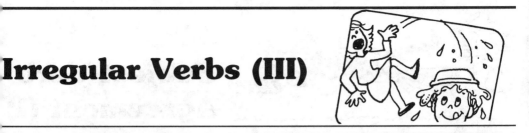

Irregular verbs do not show their past tense by adding -ed.

Circle the past tense words in the Word Box.

## Word Box

| | | | | |
|---|---|---|---|---|
| write | made | wrote | brought | slept |
| sings | sang | desk | does | dug |
| did | door | song | letter | told |

Write the past tense of the verb.

1. does
   did

2. wrote
   writes

3. sang
   sing

4. makes
   made

5. sleep
   slept

*I made a funny video.*

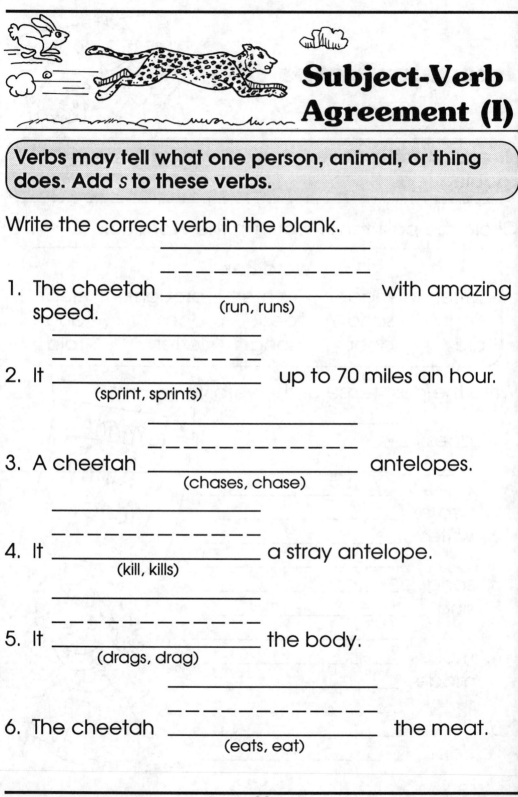

# Subject-Verb Agreement (I)

Verbs may tell what one person, animal, or thing does. Add *s* to these verbs.

Write the correct verb in the blank.

1. The cheetah _____ with amazing speed.
   (run, runs)

2. It _____ up to 70 miles an hour.
   (sprint, sprints)

3. A cheetah _____ antelopes.
   (chases, chase)

4. It _____ a stray antelope.
   (kill, kills)

5. It _____ the body.
   (drags, drag)

6. The cheetah _____ the meat.
   (eats, eat)

# Subject-Verb Agreement (II)

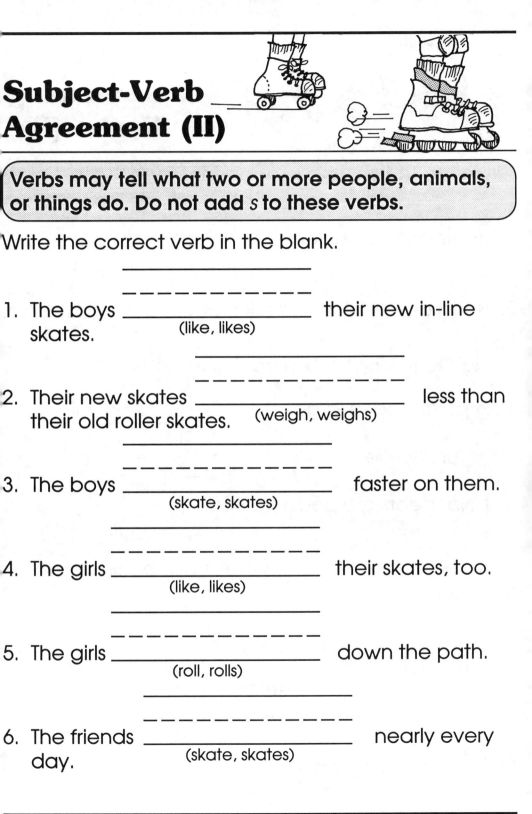

**Verbs may tell what two or more people, animals, or things do. Do not add *s* to these verbs.**

Write the correct verb in the blank.

1. The boys _____ their new in-line skates.
   (like, likes)

2. Their new skates _____ less than their old roller skates. (weigh, weighs)

3. The boys _____ faster on them.
   (skate, skates)

4. The girls _____ their skates, too.
   (like, likes)

5. The girls _____ down the path.
   (roll, rolls)

6. The friends _____ nearly every day.
   (skate, skates)

# Reviewing Verbs (I)

Circle the **action verb** in each sentence. Write it.

_____

1. Bears eat plants, fish, and insects. _____

_____

2. Bears catch fish with their claws. _____

Circle the **linking verb** in each sentence.

1. A polar bear is large.

2. Its fur is white.

3. Polar bears are good hunters.

Write the verb that shows what is happening **now** in the blank.

_____

1. The cubs _____ with their mothers.
　　　　　　　(stay, stayed)

_____

2. They _____ very fast.
　　　　(grow, grew)

# Reviewing Verbs (II)

Write the verbs that show **past** action.

1. I _____ an unusual farm.
   (visit, visited)

2. The farmer _____ ostriches.
   (raises, raised)

3. I _____ their huge eggs.
   (weighed, weighs)

4. Just one ostrich egg _____
   several people.          (feeds, fed)

Write the correct verb.

1. Ostriches _____ strange to me.
   (look, looks)

2. The teacher _____ to an ostrich.
   (points, point)

# Complete Sentences and Fragments (I)

A sentence is a group of words that tells a complete idea. It has a subject and a predicate.

Write **S** for *sentence* or **No** for *not a sentence*.

_____ 1. I took an imaginary trip to Saturn.

_____ 2. In my spaceship.

_____ 3. It took me only one day to reach the planet.

_____ 4. I saw its rings of ice-covered rocks.

_____ 5. I took pictures of its satellites.

_____ 6. About 29 $\frac{1}{2}$ earth-years to orbit the sun.

_____ 7. Maybe I'll go to Saturn next!

# Complete Sentences and Fragments (II)

| A sentence is a group of words that tells a complete idea. It has a subject and a predicate. |
| --- |

Circle the letter under **Sentence** if the words tell a complete idea. Circle the letter under **Not a Sentence** if the words do not.

| | | Sentence | Not a Sentence |
| --- | --- | --- | --- |
| 1. | Some famous pets have lived in the White House. | Y | L |
| 2. | Caroline Kennedy had a pony. | A | R |
| 3. | Also a pet named Robin. | T | A |
| 4. | President Johnson had two beagles. | N | M |
| 5. | Named Him and Her. | S | C |
| 6. | Susan Ford had a cat. | R | E |

Write the circled letters above the matching numerals to spell the answer to the question.

What kind of an animal was Robin?

a __ __ __ __ __ __
   5   2   4   3   6   1

# Subjects of Sentences (I)

The subject of a sentence tells who or what does something.

Underline the subject of each sentence.

1. My pen pal lives in Australia.

2. We write to each other often.

3. Susan's family owns a sheep ranch.

4. They live far away from cities and towns.

5. Susan has school at home.

6. She watches special classes on television.

7. The teacher and Susan talk by telephone.

8. Susan's mother and father help her also.

9. Australia is a very beautiful continent.

10. The continent is in the southern hemisphere.

# Subjects of Sentences (II)

The subject of a sentence tells who or what does something.

Underline the subject of each sentence.

1. Dogs can be more than just pets.

2. Some dogs help people in special ways.

3. Children in wheelchairs can use dogs.

4. A big dog can pull a wheelchair.

5. Dogs pick up things that are dropped.

6. A blind person may have a guide dog.

7. Guide dogs help blind people get around.

8. Deaf people use dogs as helpers, too.

9. Dogs can be taught to open doors.

10. Special dogs can be companions to almost anyone.

# Subjects of Sentences (III)

**The subject of a sentence tells who or what does something.**

Underline the subject of each sentence.

1. Fishing is always fun.

2. Grandpa packs a lunch to take along.

3. We get our rods and reels.

4. The tackle box is heavy to carry.

5. The bait is in the bucket.

6. The pond is just over the hill.

7. I hope to have good luck today.

8. The weather couldn't be better.

Write a subject to complete each sentence.

1. _____ jumped out of the water.

2. _____ reeled in a fish.

# Answer Key
## Grammar
### Grade 2

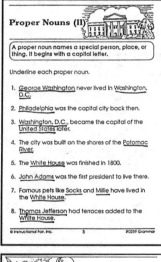

**Common Nouns (I)**

A common noun names a person, place, or thing.

Fill in the circle below each common noun.

1. The boy took a bucket to the beach.
2. His sister took a pail and a big umbrella.
3. The children set their things on the sand.
4. Then they began to build a sand castle.
5. Other people waded in the surf.
6. Two men flew big box kites.
7. The lifeguard sat on a tall stand.
8. It was a perfect day at the shore.

© Instructional Fair, Inc.    2    IF0259 Grammar

---

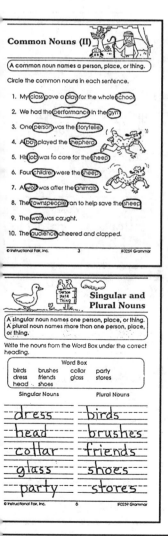

**Common Nouns (II)**

A common noun names a person, place, or thing.

Circle the common nouns in each sentence.

1. My (class) gave a (play) for the whole (school).
2. We had the (performance) in the (gym).
3. One (person) was the (storyteller).
4. A (boy) played the (shepherd).
5. His (job) was to care for the (sheep).
6. Four (children) were the (sheep).
7. A (wolf) was after the (animals).
8. The (townspeople) ran to help save the (sheep).
9. The (wolf) was caught.
10. The (audience) cheered and clapped.

© Instructional Fair, Inc.    3    IF0259 Grammar

---

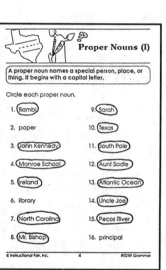

**Proper Nouns (I)**

A proper noun names a special person, place, or thing. It begins with a capital letter.

Circle each proper noun.

1. (Bambi)
2. paper
3. (John Kennedy)
4. (Monroe School)
5. (Ireland)
6. library
7. (North Carolina)
8. (Mr. Bishop)
9. (Sarah)
10. (Texas)
11. (South Pole)
12. (Aunt Sadie)
13. (Atlantic Ocean)
14. (Uncle Joe)
15. (Pecos River)
16. principal

© Instructional Fair, Inc.    4    IF0259 Grammar

---

**Proper Nouns (II)**

A proper noun names a special person, place, or thing. It begins with a capital letter.

Underline each proper noun.

1. <u>George Washington</u> never lived in <u>Washington, D.C.</u>
2. <u>Philadelphia</u> was the capital city back then.
3. <u>Washington, D.C.</u>, became the capital of the <u>United States</u> later.
4. The city was built on the shores of the <u>Potomac River</u>.
5. The <u>White House</u> was finished in 1800.
6. <u>John Adams</u> was the first president to live there.
7. Famous pets like <u>Socks</u> and <u>Millie</u> have lived in the <u>White House</u>.
8. <u>Thomas Jefferson</u> had terraces added to the <u>White House</u>.

© Instructional Fair, Inc.    5    IF0259 Grammar

---

**Singular and Plural Nouns**

A singular noun names one person, place, or thing. A plural noun names more than one person, place, or thing.

Write the nouns from the Word Box under the correct heading.

**Word Box**

birds, brushes, collar, party, dress, friends, glass, stores, head, shoes

| Singular Nouns | Plural Nouns |
| --- | --- |
| dress | birds |
| head | brushes |
| collar | friends |
| glass | shoes |
| party | stores |

© Instructional Fair, Inc.    6    IF0259 Grammar

---

**Plural Nouns (I)**

A plural noun names more than one person, place, or thing. Add s to make most singular nouns plural.

Add s to each noun to make it plural.

1. barn — barns
2. door — doors
3. horse — horses
4. painter — painters
5. star — stars
6. shovel — shovels
7. turtle — turtles
8. violin — violins

© Instructional Fair, Inc.    7    IF0259 Grammar

---

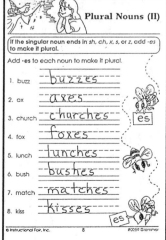

**Plural Nouns (II)**

If the singular noun ends in sh, ch, x, s, or z, add -es to make it plural.

Add -es to each noun to make it plural.

1. buzz — buzzes
2. ax — axes
3. church — churches
4. fox — foxes
5. lunch — lunches
6. bush — bushes
7. match — matches
8. kiss — kisses

© Instructional Fair, Inc.    8    IF0259 Grammar

---

© Instructional Fair, Inc.      IF0259 Grammar

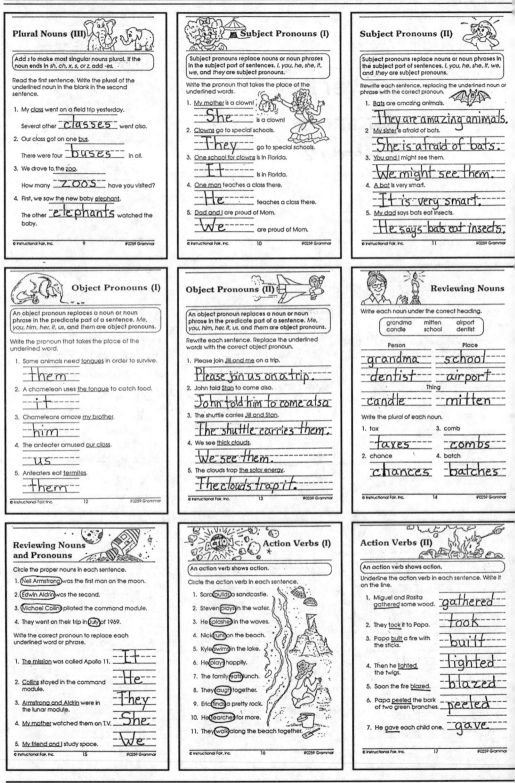

## Plural Nouns (III)

Add *s* to make most singular nouns plural. If the noun ends in *sh, ch, x, s, or z*, add *-es*.

Read the first sentence. Write the plural of the underlined noun in the blank in the second sentence.

1. My <u>class</u> went on a field trip yesterday.

   Several other **classes** went also.

2. Our class got on one <u>bus</u>.

   There were four **buses** in all.

3. We drove to the <u>zoo</u>.

   How many **zoos** have you visited?

4. First, we saw the new baby <u>elephant</u>.

   The other **elephants** watched the baby.

© Instructional Fair, Inc.    9    IF0259 Grammar

## Subject Pronouns (I)

Subject pronouns replace nouns or noun phrases in the subject part of sentences. *I, you, he, she, it, we,* and *they* are subject pronouns.

Write the pronoun that takes the place of the underlined words.

1. <u>My mother</u> is a clown!

   **She** is a clown!

2. <u>Clowns</u> go to special schools.

   **They** go to special schools.

3. <u>One school for clowns</u> is in Florida.

   **It** is in Florida.

4. <u>One man</u> teaches a class there.

   **He** teaches a class there.

5. <u>Dad and I</u> are proud of Mom.

   **We** are proud of Mom.

© Instructional Fair, Inc.    10    IF0259 Grammar

## Subject Pronouns (II)

Subject pronouns replace nouns or noun phrases in the subject part of sentences. *I, you, he, she, it,* and *they* are subject pronouns.

Rewrite each sentence, replacing the underlined noun or phrase with the correct pronoun.

1. <u>Bats</u> are amazing animals.

   **They are amazing animals.**

2. <u>My sister</u> is afraid of bats.

   **She is afraid of bats.**

3. <u>You and I</u> might see them.

   **We might see them.**

4. <u>A bat</u> is very smart.

   **It is very smart.**

5. <u>My dad</u> says bats eat insects.

   **He says bats eat insects.**

© Instructional Fair, Inc.    11    IF0259 Grammar

## Object Pronouns (I)

An object pronoun replaces a noun or noun phrase in the predicate part of a sentence. *Me, you, him, her, it, us,* and *them* are object pronouns.

Write the pronoun that takes the place of the underlined word.

1. Some animals need <u>tongues</u> in order to survive.

   **them**

2. A chameleon uses <u>the tongue</u> to catch food.

   **it**

3. Chameleons amaze <u>my brother</u>.

   **him**

4. The anteater amused <u>our class</u>.

   **us**

5. Anteaters eat <u>termites</u>.

   **them**

© Instructional Fair, Inc.    12    IF0259 Grammar

## Object Pronouns (II)

An object pronoun replaces a noun or noun phrase in the predicate part of a sentence. *Me, you, him, her, it, us,* and *them* are object pronouns.

Rewrite each sentence. Replace the underlined words with the correct object pronoun.

1. Please join <u>Jill and me</u> on a trip.

   **Please join us on a trip.**

2. John told <u>Stan</u> to come also.

   **John told him to come also.**

3. The shuttle carries <u>Jill and Stan</u>.

   **The shuttle carries them.**

4. We see <u>thick clouds</u>.

   **We see them.**

5. The clouds trap <u>the solar energy</u>.

   **The clouds trap it.**

© Instructional Fair, Inc.    13    IF0259 Grammar

## Reviewing Nouns

Write each noun under the correct heading.

| grandma | mitten | airport |
| candle | school | dentist |

| Person | Place |
| --- | --- |
| **grandma** | **school** |
| **dentist** | **airport** |

| Thing |
| --- |
| **candle** | **mitten** |

Write the plural of each noun.

1. tax    **taxes**    3. comb    **combs**

2. chance    **chances**    4. batch    **batches**

© Instructional Fair, Inc.    14    IF0259 Grammar

## Reviewing Nouns and Pronouns

Circle the proper nouns in each sentence.

1. (Neil Armstrong) was the first man on the moon.

2. (Edwin Aldrin) was the second.

3. (Michael Collins) piloted the command module.

4. They went on their trip in (July) of 1969.

Write the correct pronoun to replace each underlined word or phrase.

1. <u>The mission</u> was called Apollo 11.    **It**

2. <u>Collins</u> stayed in the command module.    **He**

3. <u>Armstrong and Aldrin</u> were in the lunar module.    **They**

4. <u>My mother</u> watched them on T.V.    **She**

5. <u>My friend and I</u> study space.    **We**

© Instructional Fair, Inc.    15    IF0259 Grammar

## Action Verbs (I)

An action verb shows action.

Circle the action verb in each sentence.

1. Sara (builds) a sandcastle.

2. Steven (plays) in the water.

3. He (splashes) in the waves.

4. Nick (runs) on the beach.

5. Kyle (swims) in the lake.

6. He (plays) happily.

7. The family (eats) lunch.

8. They (laugh) together.

9. Eric (finds) a pretty rock.

10. He (searches) for more.

11. They (walk) along the beach together.

© Instructional Fair, Inc.    16    IF0259 Grammar

## Action Verbs (II)

An action verb shows action.

Underline the action verb in each sentence. Write it on the line.

1. Miguel and Rosita <u>gathered</u> some wood.    **gathered**

2. They <u>took</u> it to Papa.    **took**

3. Papa <u>built</u> a fire with the sticks.    **built**

4. Then he <u>lighted</u> the twigs.    **lighted**

5. Soon the fire <u>blazed</u>.    **blazed**

6. Papa <u>peeled</u> the bark of two green branches.    **peeled**

7. He <u>gave</u> each child one.    **gave**

© Instructional Fair, Inc.    17    IF0259 Grammar

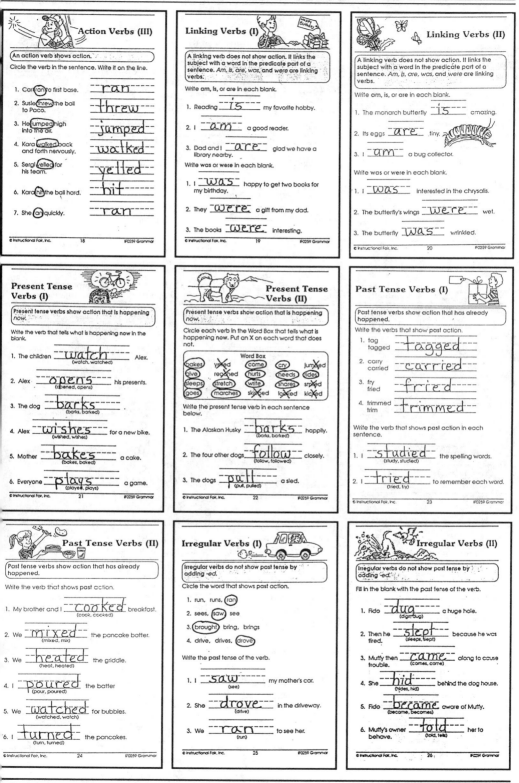

## Action Verbs (III)

An action verb shows action.

Circle the verb in the sentence. Write it on the line.

1. Carl ran to first base. — **ran**
2. Susie threw the ball to Paco. — **threw**
3. He jumped high into the air. — **jumped**
4. Kara walked back and forth nervously. — **walked**
5. Sergi yelled for his team. — **yelled**
6. Kara hit the ball hard. — **hit**
7. She ran quickly. — **ran**

© Instructional Fair, Inc.　　18　　IF0259 Grammar

## Linking Verbs (I)

A linking verb does not show action. It links the subject with a word in the predicate part of a sentence. Am, is, are, was, and were are linking verbs.

Write am, is, or are in each blank.

1. Reading __is__ my favorite hobby.
2. I __am__ a good reader.
3. Dad and I __are__ glad we have a library nearby.

Write was or were in each blank.

1. I __was__ happy to get two books for my birthday.
2. They __were__ a gift from my dad.
3. The books __were__ interesting.

© Instructional Fair, Inc.　　19　　IF0259 Grammar

## Linking Verbs (II)

A linking verb does not show action. It links the subject with a word in the predicate part of a sentence. Am, is, are, was, and were are linking verbs.

Write am, is, or are in each blank.

1. The monarch butterfly __is__ amazing.
2. Its eggs __are__ tiny.
3. I __am__ a bug collector.

Write was or were in each blank.

1. I __was__ interested in the chrysalis.
2. The butterfly's wings __were__ wet.
3. The butterfly __was__ wrinkled.

© Instructional Fair, Inc.　　20　　IF0259 Grammar

## Present Tense Verbs (I)

Present tense verbs show action that is happening now.

Write the verb that tells what is happening now in the blank.

1. The children __watch__ Alex. (watch, watched)
2. Alex __opens__ his presents. (opened, opens)
3. The dog __barks__. (barks, barked)
4. Alex __wishes__ for a new bike. (wished, wishes)
5. Mother __bakes__ a cake. (bakes, baked)
6. Everyone __plays__ a game. (played, plays)

© Instructional Fair, Inc.　　21　　IF0259 Grammar

## Present Tense Verbs (II)

Present tense verbs show action that is happening now.

Circle each verb in the Word Box that tells what is happening now. Put an X on each word that does not.

Word Box

bakes　yelled　come　cry　jumped
dive　reached　hurts　needs　rides
sleeps　stretch　write　shares　smiled
goes　marches　skipped　looked　kicked

Write the present tense verb in each sentence below.

1. The Alaskan Husky __barks__ happily. (barks, barked)
2. The four other dogs __follow__ closely. (follow, followed)
3. The dogs __pull__ a sled. (puff, pulled)

© Instructional Fair, Inc.　　22　　IF0259 Grammar

## Past Tense Verbs (I)

Past tense verbs show action that has already happened.

Write the verbs that show past action.

1. tag / tagged — **tagged**
2. carry / carried — **carried**
3. fry / fried — **fried**
4. trimmed / trim — **trimmed**

Write the verb that shows past action in each sentence.

1. I __studied__ the spelling words. (study, studied)
2. I __tried__ to remember each word. (tried, try)

© Instructional Fair, Inc.　　23　　IF0259 Grammar

## Past Tense Verbs (II)

Past tense verbs show action that has already happened.

Write the verb that shows past action.

1. My brother and I __cooked__ breakfast. (cook, cooked)
2. We __mixed__ the pancake batter. (mixed, mix)
3. We __heated__ the griddle. (heat, heated)
4. I __poured__ the batter. (pour, poured)
5. We __watched__ for bubbles. (watched, watch)
6. I __turned__ the pancakes. (turn, turned)

© Instructional Fair, Inc.　　24　　IF0259 Grammar

## Irregular Verbs (I)

Irregular verbs do not show past tense by adding -ed.

Circle the word that shows past action.

1. run, runs, ran
2. sees, saw, see
3. brought, bring, brings
4. drive, drives, drove

Write the past tense of the verb.

1. I __saw__ my mother's car. (see)
2. She __drove__ in the driveway. (drive)
3. We __ran__ to see her. (run)

© Instructional Fair, Inc.　　25　　IF0259 Grammar

## Irregular Verbs (II)

Irregular verbs do not show past tense by adding -ed.

Fill in the blank with the past tense of the verb.

1. Fido __dug__ a huge hole. (digs, bug)
2. Then he __slept__ because he was tired. (sleeps, slept)
3. Muffy then __came__ along to cause trouble. (comes, came)
4. She __hid__ behind the dog house. (rides, hid)
5. Fido __became__ aware of Muffy. (became, becomes)
6. Muffy's owner __told__ her to behave. (told, tells)

© Instructional Fair, Inc.　　26　　IF0259 Grammar

© Instructional Fair, Inc.　　　　IF0259 Grammar

## Irregular Verbs (III)

Irregular verbs do not show their past tense by adding -ed.

Circle the past tense words in the Word Box.

**Word Box**

write (made) (wrote) (brought) (slept)
sings (sang) desk (does) letter
(did) door song (told) (dug)

Write the past tense of the verb.

I wrote a funny video.

1. does
   did — **did**

2. wrote
   writes — **wrote**

3. song
   sing — **sang**

4. makes
   made — **made**

5. sleep
   slept — **slept**

© Instructional Fair, Inc.    27    IF0259 Grammar

---

## Subject-Verb Agreement (I)

Verbs may tell what one person, animal, or thing does. Add s to these verbs.

Write the correct verb in the blank.

1. The cheetah **runs** with amazing speed.
   (run, runs)

2. It **sprints** up to 70 miles an hour.
   (sprint, sprints)

3. A cheetah **chases** antelopes.
   (chases, chase)

4. It **kills** a stray antelope.
   (kill, kills)

5. It **drags** the body.
   (drags, drag)

6. The cheetah **eats** the meat.
   (eats, eat)

© Instructional Fair, Inc.    28    IF0259 Grammar

---

## Subject-Verb Agreement (II)

Verbs may tell what two or more people, animals, or things do. Do not add s to these verbs.

Write the correct verb in the blank.

1. The boys **like** their new in-line skates.
   (like, likes)

2. Their new skates **weigh** less than their old roller skates.
   (weight, weighs)

3. The boys **skate** faster on them.
   (skate, skates)

4. The girls **like** their skates, too.
   (like, likes)

5. The girls **roll** down the path.
   (roll, rolls)

6. The friends **skate** nearly every day.
   (skate, skates)

© Instructional Fair, Inc.    29    IF0259 Grammar

---

## Reviewing Verbs (I)

Circle the action verb in each sentence. Write it.

1. Bears (eat) plants, fish, and insects. **eat**

2. Bears (catch) fish with their claws. **catch**

Circle the linking verb in each sentence.

1. A polar bear (is) large.

2. Its fur (is) white.

3. Polar bears (are) good hunters.

Write the verb that shows what is happening now in the blank.

1. The cubs **stay** with their mothers.
   (stay, stayed)

2. They **grow** very fast.
   (grow, grew)

© Instructional Fair, Inc.    30    IF0259 Grammar

---

## Reviewing Verbs (II)

Write the verbs that show past action.

1. I **visited** an unusual farm.
   (visit, visited)

2. The farmer **raised** ostriches.
   (raises, raised)

3. I **weighed** their huge eggs.
   (weighed, weighs)

4. Just one ostrich egg **fed** several people.
   (feeds, fed)

Write the correct verb.

1. Ostriches **look** strange to me.
   (look, looks)

2. The teacher **points** to an ostrich.
   (points, point)

© Instructional Fair, Inc.    31    IF0259 Grammar

---

## Complete Sentences and Fragments (I)

A sentence is a group of words that tells a complete idea. It has a subject and a predicate.

Write S for sentence or No for not a sentence.

**S** 1. I took an imaginary trip to Saturn.

**No** 2. In my spaceship.

**S** 3. It took me only one day to reach the planet.

**S** 4. I saw its rings of ice-covered rocks.

**S** 5. I took pictures of its satellites.

**No** 6. About 29½ earth-years to orbit the sun.

**S** 7. Maybe I'll go to Saturn next!

© Instructional Fair, Inc.    32    IF0259 Grammar

---

## Complete Sentences and Fragments (II)

A sentence is a group of words that tells a complete idea. It has a subject and a predicate.

Circle the letter under Sentence if the words tell a complete idea. Circle the letter under Not a Sentence if the words do not.

|  | Sentence | Not a Sentence |
|---|---|---|
| 1. Some famous pets have lived in the White House. | (Y) | L |
| 2. Caroline Kennedy had a pony. | (A) | R |
| 3. Also a pet named Robin. | T | (A) |
| 4. President Johnson had two beagles. | (N) | M |
| 5. Named Him and Her. | S | (C) |
| 6. Susan Ford had a cat. | (R) | E |

Write the circled letters above the matching numerals to spell the answer to the question.

What kind of an animal was Robin?

a **C A N A R Y**
   5  2  4  3  6  1

© Instructional Fair, Inc.    33    IF0259 Grammar

---

## Subjects of Sentences (I)

The subject of a sentence tells who or what does something.

Underline the subject of each sentence.

1. My pen pal lives in Australia.

2. We write to each other often.

3. Susan's family owns a sheep ranch.

4. They live far away from cities and towns.

5. Susan has school at home.

6. She watches special classes on television.

7. The teacher and Susan talk by telephone.

8. Susan's mother and father help her also.

9. Australia is a very beautiful continent.

10. The continent is in the southern hemisphere.

© Instructional Fair, Inc.    34    IF0259 Grammar

---

## Subjects of Sentences (II)

The subject of a sentence tells who or what does something.

Underline the subject of each sentence.

1. Dogs can be more than just pets.

2. Some dogs help people in special ways.

3. Children in wheelchairs can use dogs.

4. A big dog can pull a wheelchair.

5. Dogs pick up things that are dropped.

6. A blind person may have a guide dog.

7. Guide dogs help blind people get around.

8. Deaf people use dogs as helpers, too.

9. Dogs can be taught to open doors.

10. Special dogs can be companions to almost anyone.

© Instructional Fair, Inc.    35    IF0259 Grammar

---

© Instructional Fair, Inc.    IF0259 Gramma

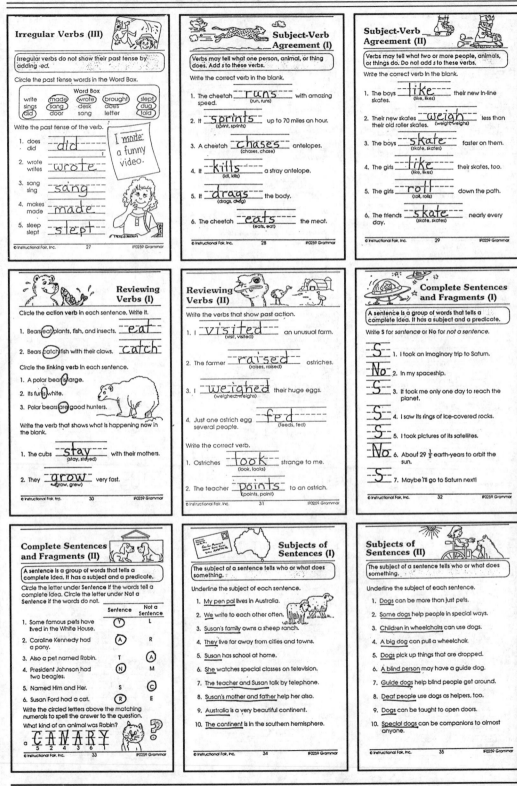

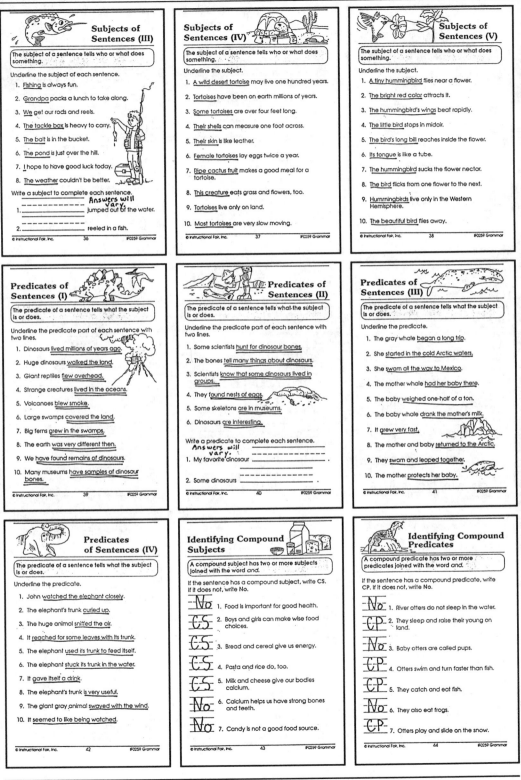

## Subjects of Sentences (III)

The subject of a sentence tells who or what does something.

Underline the subject of each sentence.

1. Fishing is always fun.
2. Grandpa packs a lunch to take along.
3. We get our rods and reels.
4. The tackle box is heavy to carry.
5. The bait is in the bucket.
6. The pond is just over the hill.
7. I hope to have good luck today.
8. The weather couldn't be better.

Write a subject to complete each sentence.

Answers will vary.

1. _____ jumped out of the water.
2. _____ reeled in a fish.

© Instructional Fair, Inc.　　36　　IF0259 Grammar

## Subjects of Sentences (IV)

The subject of a sentence tells who or what does something.

Underline the subject.

1. A wild desert tortoise may live one hundred years.
2. Tortoises have been on earth millions of years.
3. Some tortoises are over four feet long.
4. Their shells can measure one foot across.
5. Their skin is like leather.
6. Female tortoises lay eggs twice a year.
7. Ripe cactus fruit makes a good meal for a tortoise.
8. This creature eats grass and flowers, too.
9. Tortoises live only on land.
10. Most tortoises are very slow moving.

© Instructional Fair, Inc.　　37　　IF0259 Grammar

## Subjects of Sentences (V)

The subject of a sentence tells who or what does something.

Underline the subject.

1. A tiny hummingbird flies near a flower.
2. The bright red color attracts it.
3. The hummingbird's wings beat rapidly.
4. The little bird stops in midair.
5. The bird's long bill reaches inside the flower.
6. Its tongue is like a tube.
7. The hummingbird sucks the flower nectar.
8. The bird flicks from one flower to the next.
9. Hummingbirds live only in the Western Hemisphere.
10. The beautiful bird flies away.

© Instructional Fair, Inc.　　38　　IF0259 Grammar

## Predicates of Sentences (I)

The predicate of a sentence tells what the subject is or does.

Underline the predicate part of each sentence with two lines.

1. Dinosaurs lived millions of years ago.
2. Huge dinosaurs walked the land.
3. Giant reptiles flew overhead.
4. Strange creatures lived in the oceans.
5. Volcanoes blew smoke.
6. Large swamps covered the land.
7. Big ferns grew in the swamps.
8. The earth was very different then.
9. We have found remains of dinosaurs.
10. Many museums have samples of dinosaur bones.

© Instructional Fair, Inc.　　39　　IF0259 Grammar

## Predicates of Sentences (II)

The predicate of a sentence tells what the subject is or does.

Underline the predicate part of each sentence with two lines.

1. Some scientists hunt for dinosaur bones.
2. The bones tell many things about dinosaurs.
3. Scientists know that some dinosaurs lived in groups.
4. They found nests of eggs.
5. Some skeletons are in museums.
6. Dinosaurs are interesting.

Write a predicate to complete each sentence.

Answers will vary.

1. My favorite dinosaur _____ .
2. Some dinosaurs _____ .

© Instructional Fair, Inc.　　40　　IF0259 Grammar

## Predicates of Sentences (III)

The predicate of a sentence tells what the subject is or does.

Underline the predicate.

1. The gray whale began a long trip.
2. She started in the cold Arctic waters.
3. She swam all the way to Mexico.
4. The mother whale had her baby there.
5. The baby weighed one-half of a ton.
6. The baby whale drank the mother's milk.
7. It grew very fast.
8. The mother and baby returned to the Arctic.
9. They swam and leaped together.
10. The mother protects her baby.

© Instructional Fair, Inc.　　41　　IF0259 Grammar

## Predicates of Sentences (IV)

The predicate of a sentence tells what the subject is or does.

Underline the predicate.

1. John watched the elephant closely.
2. The elephant's trunk curled up.
3. The huge animal sniffed the air.
4. It reached for some leaves with its trunk.
5. The elephant used its trunk to feed itself.
6. The elephant stuck its trunk in the water.
7. It gave itself a drink.
8. The elephant's trunk is very useful.
9. The giant gray animal swayed with the wind.
10. It seemed to like being watched.

© Instructional Fair, Inc.　　42　　IF0259 Grammar

## Identifying Compound Subjects

A compound subject has two or more subjects joined with the word and.

If the sentence has a compound subject, write CS. If it does not, write No.

No 1. Food is important for good health.
CS 2. Boys and girls can make wise food choices.
CS 3. Bread and cereal give us energy.
CS 4. Pasta and rice do, too.
CS 5. Milk and cheese give our bodies calcium.
No 6. Calcium helps us have strong bones and teeth.
No 7. Candy is not a good food source.

© Instructional Fair, Inc.　　43　　IF0259 Grammar

## Identifying Compound Predicates

A compound predicate has two or more predicates joined with the word and.

If the sentence has a compound predicate, write CP. If it does not, write No.

No 1. River otters do not sleep in the water.
CP 2. They sleep and raise their young on land.
No 3. Baby otters are called pups.
CP 4. Otters swim and turn faster than fish.
CP 5. They catch and eat fish.
No 6. They also eat frogs.
CP 7. Otters play and slide on the snow.

© Instructional Fair, Inc.　　44　　IF0259 Grammar

## Statements (I)

A statement is a sentence that tells something. It begins with a capital letter and ends with a period.

If the sentence is a statement, write S on the line and add a period. If it is not, write No.

**S** 1. I went to New York City last year.
**S** 2. It is the largest city in the United States.
**No** 3. Have you ever visited there
**S** 4. I went with my family.
**S** 5. We saw the Empire State Building.
**No** 6. Did you walk through Central Park
**S** 7. I looked at the dinosaurs in the museum.

## Statements (II)

A statement is a sentence that tells something. It begins with a capital letter and ends with a period.

If the sentence is a statement, write S on the line and add a period. If it is not, write No.

**S** 1. My class made windsocks in art class.
**No** 2. Do you know what they are
**S** 3. People hang them outdoors.
**S** 4. Windsocks show the wind direction.
**S** 5. I decorated a cardboard strip.
**S** 6. I made it into a band.
**No** 7. Did you add material to blow in the wind

## Questions (I)

A question is a sentence that asks something. It begins with a capital letter and ends with a question mark.

If the sentence is a question, write Q on the line and add a question mark. If it is not, write No.

**Q** 1. How far is it to the moon?
**No** 2. It's about 225,000 miles from earth
**Q** 3. Does the moon reflect the sun's light?
**Q** 4. Why does the moon change shape?
**Q** 5. Is there gravity on the moon?
**Q** 6. Can anything grow there?
**Q** 7. Is there really a man on the moon?

## Questions (II)

A question is a sentence that asks something. It begins with a capital letter and ends with a question mark.

Write each question correctly.

1. is earth a planet
   *Is earth a planet?*
2. how far is it from the sun
   *How far is it from the sun?*
3. is it about 93 million miles
   *Is it about 93 million miles?*
4. does the earth orbit the sun
   *Does the earth orbit the sun?*
5. is the earth always spinning
   *Is the earth always spinning?*
6. how large is the earth
   *How large is the earth?*

## Exclamations

An exclamation is a sentence that shows strong feeling. It begins with a capital letter and ends with an exclamation mark.

Rewrite each exclamation correctly.

1. what an exciting day I had
   *What an exciting day I had!*
2. I won first prize
   *I won first prize!*
3. the prize is a trip
   *The prize is a trip!*
4. I can hardly wait
   *I can hardly wait!*
5. this is great
   *This is great!*
6. I'm thrilled
   *I'm thrilled!*

## Commands

A command is a sentence that tells someone to do something. The subject, you, is usually not written or spoken. A command begins with a capital letter and ends with a period.

If the sentence is a command, write C on the line and add a period. If it is not, write No.

**C** 1. Help save the environment.
**C** 2. Recycle aluminum cans.
**C** 3. Do not use paper towels or napkins.
**No** 4. Will you plant a tree
**C** 5. Use a thermos and lunchbox.
**C** 6. Turn off lights you are not using.
**No** 7. Do you compost your leaves

## Four Kinds of Sentences (I)

A statement tells something. A question asks something. An exclamation shows strong feeling. A command tells someone to do something.

Identify the sentences. Write 1 for statement, 2 for question, 3 for exclamation, or 4 for command.

**1** 1. Christopher Columbus was born in Genoa, Italy.
**2** 2. Did he want to become a sailor?
**1** 3. He worked in his father's weaving shop.
**2** 4. Did his father let him go to sea?
**1** 5. Years later he sailed for the East Indies.
**3** 6. What a voyage!
**4** 7. Find out more about Columbus.

## Four Kinds of Sentences (II)

A statement tells something. A question asks something. An exclamation shows strong feeling. A command tells someone to do something.

Identify the sentences. Write 1 for statement, 2 for question, 3 for exclamation, or 4 for command.

**3** 1. That animal changed color!
**2** 2. Have you ever heard of such a thing?
**1** 3. A chameleon is such an animal.
**4** 4. Watch it grab an insect.
**1** 5. Chameleons are slow-moving lizards.
**2** 6. Did you see its tongue?
**4** 7. Name other lizards.

## Word Order in Sentences

When the order of the words in a sentence changes, the meaning of the sentence often changes.

Change the word order to make each statement into a question and each question into a statement. Write the new sentence on the line.

1. Are bats mammals?
   *Bats are mammals.*
2. These mammals can fly.
   *Can these mammals fly?*
3. Do bats feed at night?
   *Bats do feed at night.*
4. I can find them in a cave.
   *Can I find them in a cave?*
5. I could go into the cave.
   *Could I go into the cave?*

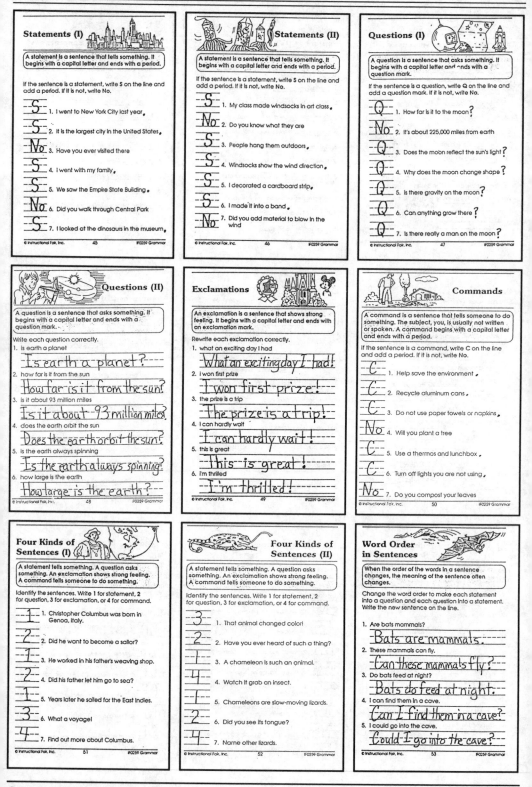

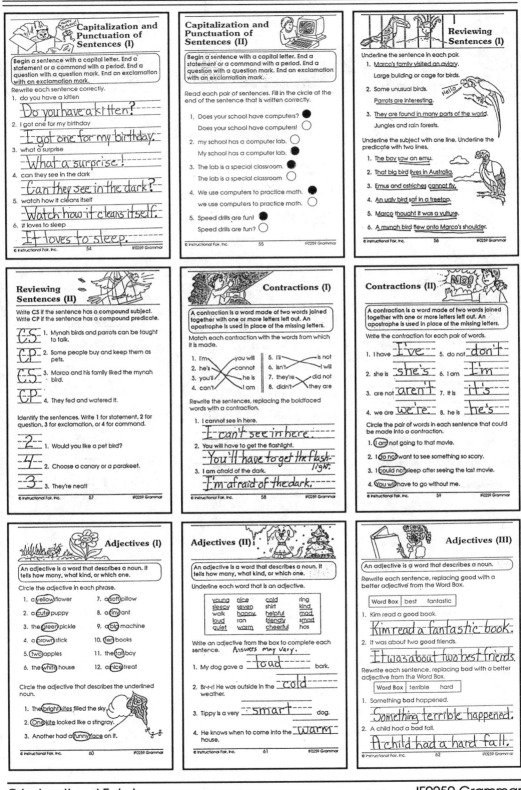

## Capitalization and Punctuation of Sentences (I)

Begin a sentence with a capital letter. End a statement or a command with a period. End a question with a question mark. End an exclamation with an exclamation mark.

Rewrite each sentence correctly.

1. do you have a kitten
   Do you have a kitten?

2. i got one for my birthday
   I got one for my birthday.

3. what a surprise
   What a surprise!

4. can they see in the dark
   Can they see in the dark?

5. watch how it cleans itself
   Watch how it cleans itself.

6. it loves to sleep
   It loves to sleep.

© Instructional Fair, Inc.      54      IF0259 Grammar

## Capitalization and Punctuation of Sentences (II)

Begin a sentence with a capital letter. End a statement or a command with a period. End a question with a question mark. End an exclamation with an exclamation mark.

Read each pair of sentences. Fill in the circle at the end of the sentence that is written correctly.

1. Does your school have computers? ●
   Does your school have computers! ○

2. my school has a computer lab. ○
   My school has a computer lab. ●

3. The lab is a special classroom. ●
   The lab is a special classroom ○

4. We use computers to practice math. ●
   we use computers to practice math. ○

5. Speed drills are fun! ●
   Speed drills are fun? ○

© Instructional Fair, Inc.      55      IF0259 Grammar

## Reviewing Sentences (I)

Underline the sentence in each pair.

1. Marco's family visited an aviary.
   Large building or cage for birds.

2. Some unusual birds.
   Parrots are interesting.

3. They are found in many parts of the world.
   Jungles and rain forests.

Underline the subject with one line. Underline the predicate with two lines.

1. The boy saw an emu.

2. That big bird lives in Australia.

3. Emus and ostriches cannot fly.

4. An ugly bird sat in a treetop.

5. Marco thought it was a vulture.

6. A mynah bird flew onto Marco's shoulder.

© Instructional Fair, Inc.      56      IF0259 Grammar

## Reviewing Sentences (II)

Write CS if the sentence has a compound subject.
Write CP if the sentence has a compound predicate.

CS  1. Mynah birds and parrots can be taught to talk.

CP  2. Some people buy and keep them as pets.

CS  3. Marco and his family liked the mynah bird.

CP  4. They fed and watered it.

Identify the sentences. Write 1 for statement, 2 for question, 3 for exclamation, or 4 for command.

2  1. Would you like a pet bird?

4  2. Choose a canary or a parakeet.

3  3. They're neat!

© Instructional Fair, Inc.      57      IF0259 Grammar

## Contractions (I)

A contraction is a word made of two words joined together with one or more letters left out. An apostrophe is used in place of the missing letters.

Match each contraction with the words from which it is made.

1. I'm — I am
2. he's — he is
3. you'll — you will
4. can't — cannot
5. I'll — I will
6. isn't — is not
7. they're — they are
8. didn't — did not

Rewrite the sentences, replacing the boldfaced words with a contraction.

1. I cannot see in here.
   I can't see in here.

2. You will have to get the flashlight.
   You'll have to get the flashlight.

3. I am afraid of the dark.
   I'm afraid of the dark.

© Instructional Fair, Inc.      58      IF0259 Grammar

## Contractions (II)

A contraction is a word made of two words joined together with one or more letters left out. An apostrophe is used in place of the missing letters.

Write the contraction for each pair of words.

1. I have  I've
2. she is  she's
3. are not  aren't
4. we are  we're
5. do not  don't
6. I am  I'm
7. it is  it's
8. he is  he's

Circle the pair of words in each sentence that could be made into a contraction.

1. I am not going to that movie.

2. I do not want to see something so scary.

3. I could not sleep after seeing the last movie.

4. You will have to go without me.

© Instructional Fair, Inc.      59      IF0259 Grammar

## Adjectives (I)

An adjective is a word that describes a noun. It tells how many, what kind, or which one.

Circle the adjective in each phrase.

1. a yellow flower
2. a cute puppy
3. the green pickle
4. a brown stick
5. two apples
6. the white house
7. a soft pillow
8. a tiny ant
9. a big machine
10. ten books
11. the tall boy
12. a nice treat

Circle the adjective that describes the underlined noun.

1. The bright kites filled the sky.

2. One kite looked like a stingray.

3. Another had a funny face on it.

© Instructional Fair, Inc.      60      IF0259 Grammar

## Adjectives (II)

An adjective is a word that describes a noun. It tells how many, what kind, or which one.

Underline each word that is an adjective.

| young | nice | cold | ring |
| sleepy | seven | shirt | kind |
| walk | happy | helpful | mad |
| loud | ran | friendly | smart |
| quiet | warm | cheerful | has |

Write an adjective from the box to complete each sentence. Answers may vary.

1. My dog gave a loud bark.

2. Br-r-r! He was outside in the cold weather.

3. Tippy is a very smart dog.

4. He knows when to come into the warm house.

© Instructional Fair, Inc.      61      IF0259 Grammar

## Adjectives (III)

An adjective is a word that describes a noun.

Rewrite each sentence, replacing good with a better adjective from the Word Box.

Word Box  best  fantastic

1. Kim read a good book.
   Kim read a fantastic book.

2. It was about two good friends.
   It was about two best friends.

Rewrite each sentence, replacing bad with a better adjective from the Word Box.

Word Box  terrible  hard

1. Something bad happened.
   Something terrible happened.

2. A child had a bad fall.
   A child had a hard fall.

© Instructional Fair, Inc.      62      IF0259 Grammar

© Instructional Fair, Inc.      IF0259 Grammar

## Adjectives (IV)

An adjective is a word that describes a noun. Adjectives make writing more interesting and specific.

Choose an adjective from the Word Box to describe each underlined noun. Write it on the line.

| Word Box | three | another | two |
| --- | --- | --- | --- |
| | safe | huge | |

1. The **huge** dinosaur looked real.

2. It stood on **two** legs.

3. **Another** dinosaur looked like a lizard.

4. It had **three** toes on each foot.

5. It needed a **safe** place to hide.

## Adjectives That Compare

Add -er to most adjectives to compare two nouns. Add -est to most adjectives to compare more than two nouns.

Circle the correct adjective and write it in the sentence.

1. Ron was a **faster** runner than Jerrod.
(faster, fastest)

2. Ben was the **fastest** of all.
(faster, fastest)

3. Charlie was the **slowest** runner in the whole race.
(slower, slowest)

4. He was even **slower** than me!
(slower, slowest)

5. The **longest** softball throw was thirty feet.
(longer, longest)

## Articles

A and an are special adjectives called articles. Use a before most singular nouns. Use an if the singular noun begins with a vowel or a silent h.

Write a or an in front of each noun.

1. **a** banana     5. **an** orange

2. **a** pineapple     6. **a** radish

3. **a** potato     7. **a** pear

4. **an** onion     8. **an** herb

Write a or an in the blank in front of the noun.

1. I took **an** apple in my lunch.

2. I also had **a** carrot and some celery.

3. My sandwich was **a** treat!

## Adverbs (I)

An adverb describes a verb. It tells how, when, or where.

Write how, when, or where on the line to tell how the underlined adverb describes the verb.

1. I play here. **where**

2. I play today. **when**

3. I play there. **where**

4. I play quietly. **how**

Write one of the adverbs above in each sentence.

1. The little boy played **there/here**
(where)

2. He sat **quietly** under the shade tree.
(how)

3. He wanted to be by himself **today**
(when)

## Adverbs (II)

An adverb describes a verb. It tells how, when, or where.

Circle the adverb and write it in the blank.

1. Toni ate her food **slowly**
(slowly, sorry)

2. She chewed each bite **carefully**
(carry, carefully)

3. Terry ate his dinner **quickly**
(quickly, quiet)

4. He chewed his food **rapidly**
(rapidly, reward)

5. He wanted to finish eating **soon**
(solve, soon)

6. Terry had been playing **outside**
(outside, over)

7. He wanted to go back **quickly**
(quack, quickly)

## Adverbs (III)

An adverb tells how, when, or where. It makes writing more interesting.

Choose an adverb from the Word Box to complete each sentence.

| Word Box | outside | gently | now |
| --- | --- | --- | --- |

1. The lion licked her cub **gently**. (how?)

2. The baby lion roared **outside**. (where?)

3. It wanted its dinner **now**. (when?)

| Word Box | carefully | around | soon |
| --- | --- | --- | --- |

1. The little fawn looked **around**. (where?)

2. Its mother listened **carefully**. (how?)

3. The mother **soon** guided her fawn into the forest. (when?)

## Adjectives and Adverbs

An adjective describes a noun or pronoun. An adverb describes a verb.

If the underlined word is used as an adjective, write ADJ on the line. If it is used as an adverb, write ADV on the line.

**ADV** 1. Dave went to the zoo yesterday.

**ADJ** 2. He was excited.

**ADV** 3. An elephant had just been born.

**ADV** 4. The baby and its mother stayed indoors.

**ADJ** 5. The zookeepers were nervous.

**ADV** 6. The mother might reject her baby later.

**ADJ** 7. The proud mother nuzzled her baby.

## Reviewing Adjectives and Adverbs (I)

Write a or an in each blank.

1. **An** uncle of mine is a firefighter.

2. He came to my class to give **a** talk.

3. I also have **an** aunt who is a firefighter.

4. I might be **a** firefighter when I grow up.

5. A firefighter is **a** courageous person.

Circle each adjective. Underline each adverb.

1. Firefighters are (brave) men and women.

2. Their work is (dangerous).

3. They fight fires everywhere.

4. Sometimes they put out fires in homes and schools.

## Reviewing Adjectives and Adverbs (II)

Write the correct form of the adjective.

1. A pygmy right whale is a **small** whale.
(small, smallest)

2. It is **smaller** than other baleen whales.
(smaller, smallest)

3. An orca is a **large** whale.
(large, larger)

4. An orca is not **larger** than a gray whale.
(larger, largest)

5. The **largest** whale is the blue whale.
(larger, largest)

Circle the adverb in each pair of words.

1. (once) one     3. (strongly) string

2. sweater (sweetly)     4. (early) east

# Subjects of Sentences (IV)

The subject of a sentence tells who or what does something.

Underline the subject.

1. A wild desert tortoise may live one hundred years.

2. Tortoises have been on earth millions of years.

3. Some tortoises are over four feet long.

4. Their shells can measure one foot across.

5. Their skin is like leather.

6. Female tortoises lay eggs twice a year.

7. Ripe cactus fruit makes a good meal for a tortoise.

8. This creature eats grass and flowers, too.

9. Tortoises live only on land.

10. Most tortoises are very slow moving.

# Subjects of Sentences (V)

The subject of a sentence tells who or what does something.

Underline the subject.

1. A tiny hummingbird flies near a flower.

2. The bright red color attracts it.

3. The hummingbird's wings beat rapidly.

4. The little bird stops in midair.

5. The bird's long bill reaches inside the flower.

6. Its tongue is like a tube.

7. The hummingbird sucks the flower nectar.

8. The bird flicks from one flower to the next.

9. Hummingbirds live only in the Western Hemisphere.

10. The beautiful bird flies away.

# Predicates of Sentences (I)

> **The predicate of a sentence tells what the subject is or does.**

Underline the predicate part of each sentence with two lines.

1. Dinosaurs lived millions of years ago.

2. Huge dinosaurs walked the land.

3. Giant reptiles flew overhead.

4. Strange creatures lived in the oceans.

5. Volcanoes blew smoke.

6. Large swamps covered the land.

7. Big ferns grew in the swamps.

8. The earth was very different then.

9. We have found remains of dinosaurs.

10. Many museums have samples of dinosaur bones.

# Predicates of Sentences (II)

> **The predicate of a sentence tells what the subject is or does.**

Underline the predicate part of each sentence with two lines.

1. Some scientists hunt for dinosaur bones.

2. The bones tell many things about dinosaurs.

3. Scientists know that some dinosaurs lived in groups.

4. They found nests of eggs.

5. Some skeletons are in museums.

6. Dinosaurs are interesting.

Write a predicate to complete each sentence.

1. My favorite dinosaur _____ .

2. Some dinosaurs _____ .

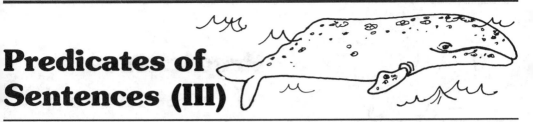

# Predicates of Sentences (III)

> The predicate of a sentence tells what the subject is or does.

Underline the predicate.

1. The gray whale began a long trip.

2. She started in the cold Arctic waters.

3. She swam all the way to Mexico.

4. The mother whale had her baby there.

5. The baby weighed one-half of a ton.

6. The baby whale drank the mother's milk.

7. It grew very fast.

8. The mother and baby returned to the Arctic.

9. They swam and leaped together.

10. The mother protects her baby.

# Predicates
## of Sentences (IV)

**The predicate of a sentence tells what the subject is or does.**

Underline the predicate.

1. John watched the elephant closely.

2. The elephant's trunk curled up.

3. The huge animal sniffed the air.

4. It reached for some leaves with its trunk.

5. The elephant used its trunk to feed itself.

6. The elephant stuck its trunk in the water.

7. It gave itself a drink.

8. The elephant's trunk is very useful.

9. The giant gray animal swayed with the wind.

10. It seemed to like being watched.

# Identifying Compound Subjects

A compound subject has two or more subjects joined with the word *and*.

If the sentence has a compound subject, write **CS**. If it does not, write **No**.

_____  1. Food is important for good health.

_____  2. Boys and girls can make wise food choices.

_____  3. Bread and cereal give us energy.

_____  4. Pasta and rice do, too.

_____  5. Milk and cheese give our bodies calcium.

_____  6. Calcium helps us have strong bones and teeth.

_____  7. Candy is not a good food source.

# Identifying Compound Predicates

A compound predicate has two or more predicates joined with the word *and*.

If the sentence has a compound predicate, write **CP**. If it does not, write **No**.

_____ 1. River otters do not sleep in the water.

_____ 2. They sleep and raise their young on land.

_____ 3. Baby otters are called pups.

_____ 4. Otters swim and turn faster than fish.

_____ 5. They catch and eat fish.

_____ 6. They also eat frogs.

_____ 7. Otters play and slide on the snow.

# Statements (I)

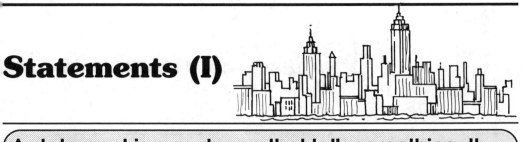

A statement is a sentence that tells something. It begins with a capital letter and ends with a period.

If the sentence is a statement, write **S** on the line and add a period. If it is not, write **No**.

_____ 1. I went to New York City last year

_____ 2. It is the largest city in the United States

_____ 3. Have you ever visited there

_____ 4. I went with my family

_____ 5. We saw the Empire State Building

_____ 6. Did you walk through Central Park

_____ 7. I looked at the dinosaurs in the museum

# Statements (II)

A statement is a sentence that tells something. It begins with a capital letter and ends with a period.

If the sentence is a statement, write **S** on the line and add a period. If it is not, write **No**.

_____ 1. My class made windsocks in art class

_____ 2. Do you know what they are

_____ 3. People hang them outdoors

_____ 4. Windsocks show the wind direction

_____ 5. I decorated a cardboard strip

_____ 6. I made it into a band

_____ 7. Did you add material to blow in the wind

# Questions (I)

A question is a sentence that asks something. It begins with a capital letter and ends with a question mark.

If the sentence is a question, write **Q** on the line and add a question mark. If it is not, write **No**.

_____ 1.  How far is it to the moon

_____ 2.  It's about 225,000 miles from earth

_____ 3.  Does the moon reflect the sun's light

_____ 4.  Why does the moon change shape

_____ 5.  Is there gravity on the moon

_____ 6.  Can anything grow there

_____ 7.  Is there really a man on the moon

A question is a sentence that asks something. It begins with a capital letter and ends with a question mark.

Write each question correctly.

1. is earth a planet

_____

2. how far is it from the sun

_____

3. is it about 93 million miles

_____

4. does the earth orbit the sun

_____

5. is the earth always spinning

_____

6. how large is the earth

_____

# Exclamations

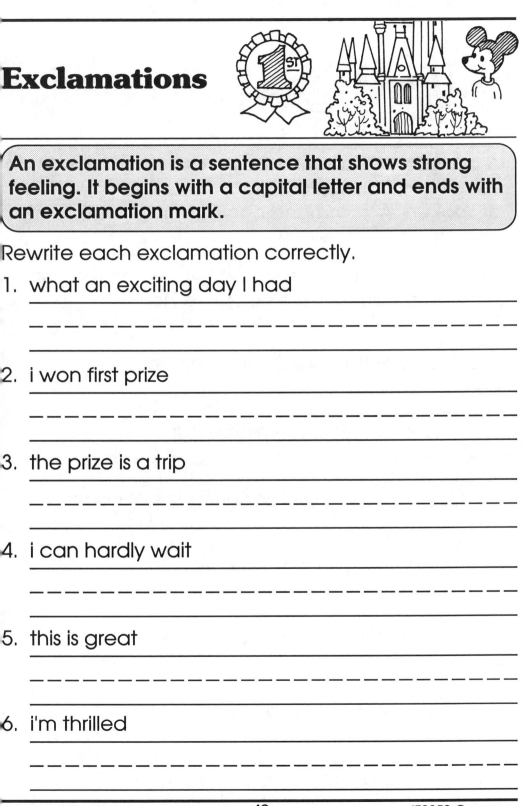

An exclamation is a sentence that shows strong feeling. It begins with a capital letter and ends with an exclamation mark.

Rewrite each exclamation correctly.

1. what an exciting day I had

   _____

   _____

2. i won first prize

   _____

   _____

3. the prize is a trip

   _____

   _____

4. i can hardly wait

   _____

   _____

5. this is great

   _____

   _____

6. i'm thrilled

   _____

   _____

# Commands

A command is a sentence that tells someone to do something. The subject, you, is usually not written or spoken. A command begins with a capital letter and ends with a period.

If the sentence is a command, write **C** on the line and add a period. If it is not, write **No**.

_____ 1. Help save the environment

_____ 2. Recycle aluminum cans

_____ 3. Do not use paper towels or napkins

_____ 4. Will you plant a tree

_____ 5. Use a thermos and lunchbox

_____ 6. Turn off lights you are not using

_____ 7. Do you compost your leaves

# Four Kinds of Sentences (I)

A statement tells something. A question asks something. An exclamation shows strong feeling. A command tells someone to do something.

Identify the sentences. Write **1** for statement, **2** for question, **3** for exclamation, or **4** for command.

_____ 1. Christopher Columbus was born in Genoa, Italy.

_____ 2. Did he want to become a sailor?

_____ 3. He worked in his father's weaving shop.

_____ 4. Did his father let him go to sea?

_____ 5. Years later he sailed for the East Indies.

_____ 6. What a voyage!

_____ 7. Find out more about Columbus.

# Four Kinds of Sentences (II)

A statement tells something. A question asks something. An exclamation shows strong feeling. A command tells someone to do something.

Identify the sentences. Write **1** for statement, **2** for question, **3** for exclamation, or **4** for command.

_____ 1. That animal changed color!

_____ 2. Have you ever heard of such a thing?

_____ 3. A chameleon is such an animal.

_____ 4. Watch it grab an insect.

_____ 5. Chameleons are slow-moving lizards.

_____ 6. Did you see its tongue?

_____ 7. Name other lizards.

# Word Order in Sentences

When the order of the words in a sentence changes, the meaning of the sentence often changes.

Change the word order to make each statement into a question and each question into a statement. Write the new sentence on the line.

1. Are bats mammals?

   _____

   _____

2. These mammals can fly.

   _____

   _____

3. Do bats feed at night?

   _____

   _____

4. I can find them in a cave.

   _____

   _____

5. I could go into the cave.

   _____

   _____

# Capitalization and Punctuation of Sentences (I)

Begin a sentence with a capital letter. End a statement or a command with a period. End a question with a question mark. End an exclamation with an exclamation mark.

Rewrite each sentence correctly.

1. do you have a kitten

_____

_____

2. i got one for my birthday

_____

_____

3. what a surprise

_____

_____

4. can they see in the dark

_____

_____

5. watch how it cleans itself

_____

_____

6. it loves to sleep

_____

_____

# Capitalization and Punctuation of Sentences (II)

Begin a sentence with a capital letter. End a statement or a command with a period. End a question with a question mark. End an exclamation with an exclamation mark.

Read each pair of sentences. Fill in the circle at the end of the sentence that is written correctly.

1. Does your school have computers? ◯

   Does your school have computers! ◯

2. my school has a computer lab. ◯

   My school has a computer lab. ◯

3. The lab is a special classroom. ◯

   The lab is a special classroom ◯

4. We use computers to practice math. ◯

   we use computers to practice math. ◯

5. Speed drills are fun! ◯

   Speed drills are fun? ◯

# Reviewing Sentences (I)

Underline the sentence in each pair.

1. Marco's family visited an aviary.

   Large building or cage for birds.

2. Some unusual birds.

   Parrots are interesting.

   *Hello*

3. They are found in many parts of the world.

   Jungles and rain forests.

Underline the subject with one line. Underline the predicate with two lines.

1. The boy saw an emu.

2. That big bird lives in Australia.

3. Emus and ostriches cannot fly.

4. An ugly bird sat in a treetop.

5. Marco thought it was a vulture.

6. A mynah bird flew onto Marco's shoulder.

# Reviewing Sentences (II)

Write **CS** if the sentence has a **compound subject**.
Write **CP** if the sentence has a **compound predicate**.

_____ 1. Mynah birds and parrots can be taught to talk.

_____ 2. Some people buy and keep them as pets.

_____ 3. Marco and his family liked the mynah bird.

_____ 4. They fed and watered it.

Identify the sentences. Write **1** for statement, **2** for question, **3** for exclamation, or **4** for command.

_____ 1. Would you like a pet bird?

_____ 2. Choose a canary or a parakeet.

_____ 3. They're neat!

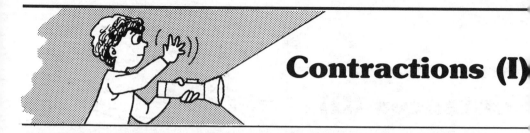

# Contractions (I)

A contraction is a word made of two words joined together with one or more letters left out. An apostrophe is used in place of the missing letters.

Match each contraction with the words from which it is made.

| | | | | | |
|---|---|---|---|---|---|
| 1. I'm | you will | | 5. I'll | | is not |
| 2. he's | cannot | | 6. isn't | | I will |
| 3. you'll | he is | | 7. they're | | did not |
| 4. can't | I am | | 8. didn't | | they are |

Rewrite the sentences, replacing the boldfaced words with a contraction.

1. I **cannot** see in here.

   _____

2. **You will** have to get the flashlight.

   _____

3. **I am** afraid of the dark.

   _____

# Contractions (II)

A contraction is a word made of two words joined together with one or more letters left out. An apostrophe is used in place of the missing letters.

Write the contraction for each pair of words.

1. I have _____    5. do not _____

2. she is _____    6. I am _____

3. are not _____    7. it is _____

4. we are _____    8. he is _____

Circle the pair of words in each sentence that could be made into a contraction.

1. I am not going to that movie.

2. I do not want to see something so scary.

3. I could not sleep after seeing the last movie.

4. You will have to go without me.

# Adjectives (I)

An adjective is a word that describes a noun. It tells how many, what kind, or which one.

Circle the adjective in each phrase.

1. a yellow flower
2. a cute puppy
3. the green pickle
4. a brown stick
5. two apples
6. the white house

7. a soft pillow
8. a tiny ant
9. a big machine
10. ten books
11. the tall boy
12. a nice treat

Circle the adjective that describes the underlined noun.

1. The bright <u>kites</u> filled the sky.

2. One <u>kite</u> looked like a stingray.

3. Another had a funny <u>face</u> on it.

# Adjectives (II)

An adjective is a word that describes a noun. It tells how many, what kind, or which one.

Underline each word that is an adjective.

| | | | |
|---|---|---|---|
| young | nice | cold | ring |
| sleepy | seven | shirt | kind |
| walk | happy | helpful | mad |
| loud | ran | friendly | smart |
| quiet | warm | cheerful | has |

Write an adjective from the box to complete each sentence.

1. My dog gave a _____ bark.

2. Br-r-r! He was outside in the _____ weather.

3. Tippy is a very _____ dog.

4. He knows when to come into the _____ house.

# Adjectives (III)

An adjective is a word that describes a noun.

Rewrite each sentence, replacing **good** with a better adjective from the Word Box.

| **Word Box** | best | fantastic |
|---|---|---|

1. Kim read a **good** book.

   _____

   _ _ _ _ _ _ _ _ _ _ _ _ _ _ _ _ _ _ _ _ _ _

   _____

2. It was about two **good** friends.

   _____

   _ _ _ _ _ _ _ _ _ _ _ _ _ _ _ _ _ _ _ _ _ _

   _____

Rewrite each sentence, replacing **bad** with a better adjective from the Word Box.

| **Word Box** | terrible | hard |
|---|---|---|

1. Something **bad** happened.

   _____

   _ _ _ _ _ _ _ _ _ _ _ _ _ _ _ _ _ _ _ _ _ _

   _____

2. A child had a **bad** fall.

   _____

   _ _ _ _ _ _ _ _ _ _ _ _ _ _ _ _ _ _ _ _ _ _

   _____

# Adjectives (IV)

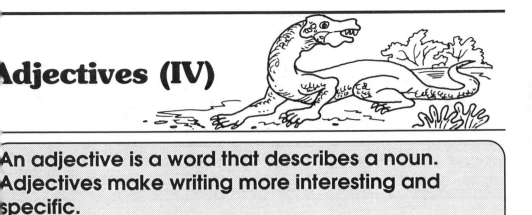

An adjective is a word that describes a noun. Adjectives make writing more interesting and specific.

Choose an adjective from the Word Box to describe each underlined noun. Write it on the line.

| Word Box | three    another    two |
|----------|-------------------------|
|          | safe      huge          |

1. The _____ <u>dinosaur</u> looked real.

2. It stood on _____ <u>legs</u>.

3. _____ <u>dinosaur</u> looked like a lizard.

4. It had _____ <u>toes</u> on each foot.

5. It needed a _____ <u>place</u> to hide.

# Adjectives That Compare

Add -er to most adjectives to compare two nouns.
Add -est to most adjectives to compare more than two nouns.

Circle the correct adjective and write it in the sentence.

1. Ron was a _____ runner than Jerrod.
   (faster, fastest)

2. Ben was the _____ of all.
   (faster, fastest)

3. Charlie was the _____ runner in the whole race.
   (slower, slowest)

4. He was even _____ than me!
   (slower, slowest)

5. The _____ softball throw was thirty feet.
   (longer, longest)

# Articles

*A* **and** *an* **are special adjectives called articles.**
**Use** *a* **before most singular nouns. Use** *an* **if the**
**singular noun begins with a vowel or a silent** *h.*

Write **a** or **an** in front of each noun.

1. _____ banana       5. _____ orange

2. _____ pineapple    6. _____ radish

3. _____ potato       7. _____ pear

4. _____ onion        8. _____ herb

Write **a** or **an** in the blank in front of the noun.

1. I took _____ apple in my lunch.

2. I also had _____ carrot and some celery.

3. My sandwich was _____ treat!

# Adverbs (I

An adverb describes a verb. It tells how, when, or where.

Write **how, when,** or **where** on the line to tell how the underlined adverb describes the verb.

1. I play <u>here</u>. _____

2. I play <u>today</u>. _____

3. I play <u>there</u>. _____

4. I play <u>quietly</u>. _____

Write one of the adverbs above in each sentence.

1. The little boy played _____
(where)

2. He sat _____ under the shade tree.
(how)

3. He wanted to be by himself _____
(when)

# Adverbs (II)

An adverb describes a verb. It tells how, when, or where.

Circle the adverb and write it in the blank.

_____

. Toni ate her food _____ .
(slowly, sorry)

. She chewed each bite _____ .
(carry, carefully)

. Terry ate his dinner _____ .
(quickly, quiet)

. He chewed his food _____ .
(rapidly, reward)

. He wanted to finish eating _____ .
(solve, soon)

. Terry had been playing _____ .
(outside, over)

. He wanted to go back _____ .
(quack, quickly)

# Adverbs (III

An adverb tells how, when, or where. It makes writing more interesting.

Choose an adverb from the Word Box to complete each sentence.

| **Word Box** | outside    gently    now |
|--------------|--------------------------|

1. The lion licked her cub _____ .(how?

2. The baby lion roared _____ . (where?

3. It wanted its dinner _____ . (when?)

| **Word Box** | carefully    around    soon |
|--------------|-----------------------------|

1. The little fawn looked _____ . (where?

2. Its mother listened _____ . (how?

3. The mother _____ guided her fawn into the forest. (when?)

# Adjectives and Adverbs

An adjective describes a noun or pronoun. An adverb describes a verb.

If the underlined word is used as an adjective, write **ADJ** on the line. If it is used as an adverb, write **ADV**.

_____ 1. Dave went to the zoo <u>yesterday</u>.

_____ 2. He was <u>excited</u>.

_____ 3. An elephant had <u>just</u> been born.

_____ 4. The baby and its mother stayed <u>indoors</u>.

_____ 5. The zookeepers were <u>nervous</u>.

_____ 6. The mother might reject her baby <u>later</u>.

_____ 7. The <u>proud</u> mother nuzzled her baby.

# Reviewing Adjectives and Adverbs (I)

Write **a** or **an** in each blank.

1. _____ uncle of mine is a firefighter.

2. He came to my class to give _____ talk.

3. I also have _____ aunt who is a firefighter.

4. I might be _____ firefighter when I grow up.

5. A firefighter is _____ courageous person.

Circle each adjective. Underline each adverb.

1. Firefighters are brave men and women.

2. Their work is dangerous.

3. They fight fires everywhere.

4. Sometimes they put out fires in homes and schools.

# Reviewing Adjectives and Adverbs (II)

Write the correct form of the adjective.

1.  A pygmy right whale is a _____ whale.
    (small, smallest)

2.  It is _____ than other baleen whales.
    (smaller, smallest)

3.  An orca is a _____ whale.
    (large, larger)

4.  An orca is not _____ than a gray whale.
    (large, larger)

5.  The _____ whale is the blue whale.
    (larger, largest)

Circle the adverb in each pair of words.

1.  once, one
2.  sweater, sweetly

3.  strongly, string
4.  early, east